IF I ONLY KNEW

Life Lessons I Wish Someone Had Told Me Earlier

NOAH WAYAN

TOP ARTISTS 4U LLC

First Printing, 2026

ISBN

Paperback - 13: 978-1-968871-81-9

Ebook - 13: 978-1-968871-82-6

Top Artists 4 U LLC

15021 Ventura Blvd. #783 Sherman Oaks, CA 91403

TopArtists4U@gmail.com

Dedication

This book is dedicated to anyone who has ever paused in the middle of an ordinary day and quietly thought to themselves - if I only knew then what I know now.

It is for the people who learned certain lessons later than they would have liked. The ones who discovered that time moves faster than expected, that some opportunities do not wait, and that the smallest choices often carry more weight than they appeared to at the time.

It is for those who are still early in their journey, standing at the beginning of decisions that will quietly shape the direction of years they have not yet lived. It is for those who are somewhere in the middle, moving through a season of life that feels uncertain or unclear, wondering whether the direction they are heading still reflects the person they are becoming. And it is for those further along, looking back with the particular kind of clarity that only experience can provide, finding in that reflection not regret but understanding - and in that understanding, the recognition that the life still ahead of them remains worth living with full intention.

If the lessons in these pages reach someone before life teaches them the hard way, then every experience behind them will have served a purpose far greater than the one it originally carried.

Because sometimes a few honest words, heard at exactly the right moment, can quietly save a person years of unnecessary struggle.
And that possibility is worth every page.

Introduction

At some point in life, almost everyone says the same sentence.
If I only knew then what I know now.

We usually say it after years have passed - after mistakes have been made, after opportunities have slipped by, and after we have accumulated enough experience to finally see clearly what we could not see when it mattered most. Life is a patient teacher, but its lessons are often expensive. Some cost time. Some cost money. Some cost relationships that deserved better. And some cost years that cannot be recovered, spent moving in a direction we never fully chose.

What makes this particularly worth examining is that most of the lessons people eventually learn are not secrets. They are not hidden inside rare experiences or available only to exceptional people. They are truths that emerge gradually as a person moves through life - sometimes at thirty, sometimes at fifty, and sometimes even later. Truths about time and how it accumulates.

About money and how it responds to behavior. About courage and what it actually costs to avoid it. About the people we surround ourselves with and how quietly they shape the direction of our thinking. About the habits we allow to form and the lives those habits eventually construct.

Many of these truths are simple. Almost obvious, in hindsight. Yet they often arrive only after we have already paid the price of learning them through experience rather than awareness.
This book is a collection of those lessons.

They are not motivational slogans designed to produce temporary excitement. They are not complicated theories that require expertise to understand. They are honest observations about the patterns that shape people's lives - patterns that repeat across different circumstances, different backgrounds, and different generations with a consistency that suggests they are worth paying attention to regardless of where a person currently finds themselves.

Each chapter examines a different dimension of life - time, responsibility, money, courage, relationships, discipline, perspective, reinvention, and the life that still remains ahead. Within each chapter, ten lessons offer specific and distinct insights designed to be read slowly and considered carefully rather than consumed quickly and forgotten.

At the close of each chapter, two reflection questions invite you to bring the ideas you have just read into contact with your own life - not abstractly, but concretely and honestly.

Some of these lessons may feel immediately familiar. Others may challenge the way you currently think about the choices you are making and the direction you are heading. A few may arrive at exactly the right moment and land in a way that is difficult to explain but impossible to ignore.

That last possibility is the one this book was written for.
Because if even one of these ideas reaches you at the right moment

- before life forces you to learn it the harder way - it could change something important. Not dramatically, perhaps. But genuinely. And over time, genuinely is more than enough.
That is the purpose of this book.

To offer the kind of honest, grounded wisdom that many people spend years wishing someone had offered them earlier. And to offer it now, while there is still plenty of time to use it.

1

The Wake-Up

Most people do not realize how fast life is moving until they pause long enough to look back.

That pause, when it comes, can be unsettling. A person looks at the years behind them and begins to notice things they could not see while they were living through them. Habits they thought were temporary had quietly become permanent. Opportunities they assumed would return never did. Decisions they treated as small turned out to matter more than expected.

This is what many people describe as a wake-up moment. It does not always arrive dramatically. Sometimes it comes quietly, in an ordinary afternoon, when a person suddenly realizes that more time has passed than they intended to let go. The wake-up moment is not a punishment. It is an invitation.

It is the moment when a person begins to see their life not as something that simply happens to them, but as something shaped daily by the choices they make. That realization can feel uncomfortable at first, because it removes the idea that circumstances alone determine outcomes. But it is also one of the most empowering realizations a person can reach, because it means that direction can always be changed.

People who experience this kind of awareness often describe it as seeing their life from the outside for the first time. They begin to recognize patterns they had been living inside of without ever questioning them. They see how their daily routines, the people they spent time with, and the decisions they repeatedly avoided all quietly added up to the life they were currently living.

What follows that recognition is a choice. A person can acknowledge what they see and allow it to deepen their intention going forward. Or they can return to the comfort of familiar patterns and allow the awareness to fade. Those who choose to stay awake to that awareness rarely regret it. Because awareness does not erase the past. But it does something equally powerful. It gives you the present.

Lesson 1 *Time is the one thing you spend whether you plan to or not.*

Every day that passes represents a portion of life that has been used. It does not matter whether that time was invested wisely or allowed to drift without purpose. Time moves forward regardless of our awareness of it. Many people assume they have endless opportunities to correct course later, only to discover that the years accumulated quietly while they were waiting. Recognizing that time is always being spent encourages us to think more carefully about how we use what remains.

Lesson 2 *Waiting for the perfect moment is how years quietly disappear.*

Many people delay important decisions believing that a better opportunity will arrive when conditions feel safer, easier, or more certain. The problem is that life continues moving during that delay, and opportunities often pass unnoticed while we wait. Progress usually begins not when circumstances are ideal, but when a person decides to move forward anyway. The perfect moment rarely comes. The right decision, made imperfectly, almost always does more than the perfect decision made too late.

Lesson 3 *The habits you repeat today are quietly building your future.*

A single decision rarely changes a life overnight, but habits repeated over months and years can reshape everything. The routines we adopt become patterns, and those patterns slowly influence our health, finances, relationships, and opportunities. What feels small and insignificant today can become deeply powerful over time. When people recognize this early, they begin paying closer attention to the habits they allow into their daily lives, understanding that each one is quietly contributing to the person they are becoming.

Lesson 4 *A wasted day rarely feels serious until it becomes a wasted decade.*

It is easy to overlook a single day that slips by without progress. After all, it is only one day. But life rarely moves in isolated moments. Days become weeks, weeks become months, and eventually those months become years. Most meaningful change happens gradually, which means that neglect accumulates just as quietly as progress does. When people look back, they often realize that long periods of time passed with little intention simply because no single day ever felt important enough to change.

Lesson 5 *Small choices compound into large consequences.*

Most major outcomes in life are not the result of one dramatic decision. Instead, they develop from repeated small choices made over time. Spending a little more than necessary, avoiding difficult conversations, postponing responsibilities, or neglecting opportunities may seem harmless in the moment. Yet when these patterns continue, they gradually shape circumstances that become difficult to reverse. Understanding this principle changes how a person thinks about even the smallest daily decisions.

Lesson 6 *Drifting through life is still a direction.*

Some people believe that avoiding decisions protects them from making mistakes. In reality, avoiding decisions simply means allowing circumstances to decide for them. When a person drifts without intention, they often end up somewhere they never planned to be, living a life shaped more by default than by choice. Choosing a direction, even an imperfect one, usually creates far more opportunity than remaining stuck in uncertainty while waiting for clarity that may never arrive on its own.

Lesson 7 *The earlier you begin improving your life, the easier progress becomes.*

Time works either for us or against us depending on when we choose to begin. When people start building healthy habits, financial discipline, and personal growth early, those improvements accumulate over many years. Waiting until later often means working harder to correct patterns that have already taken deep root. Starting early does not guarantee perfection, but it makes meaningful progress far easier to sustain. Every year of early effort becomes a foundation that the future can be built upon.

Lesson 8 *Life rarely changes overnight, but it always changes over time.*

People often expect transformation to happen quickly. They want visible results that appear almost immediately. Yet most meaningful change happens gradually, building so slowly that it is nearly invisible from day to day. The effects of learning, discipline, and consistent effort accumulate quietly until one day the difference becomes undeniable. Understanding this helps people remain patient and committed during the long, ordinary stretches of growth when progress is real but not yet visible.

Lesson 9 *Awareness is not just the first step - it is the most important one.*

Before anything improves, a person must first recognize where they currently stand. Many people move through life on autopilot, repeating habits without ever questioning whether those habits are truly serving them. They accept patterns simply because those patterns are familiar. The moment someone becomes genuinely aware of the forces shaping their life is the same moment they gain the ability to choose something different. Without awareness, change has no starting point.

Lesson 10 *The best moment to start changing your life is the moment you realize you should.*

There is rarely a perfect starting point for improvement. Waiting for motivation, certainty, or ideal conditions often leads to further delay, and further delay leads to more of the same. The most effective starting point is simply the moment when awareness appears. Once a person clearly recognizes that change is necessary, the next step becomes obvious. Not tomorrow. Not when things settle down. Now, with whatever is available, is where every meaningful change begins.

Reflection Questions:

1. What is one habit you have been repeating that, if you are honest with yourself, is not moving your life in the direction you truly want?

2. Is there a decision you have been postponing that deserves your honest attention right now — not someday, but today?

2

Taking Responsibility

There is a turning point that changes everything for a person, and it rarely arrives with fanfare.

It does not come from a new opportunity, a stroke of luck, or someone else finally stepping in to help. It comes from a quiet internal shift — the moment a person stops looking outward for explanations and begins looking inward for answers.
That shift is the acceptance of responsibility.

For many people, this realization does not arrive easily or early. It is natural, especially in younger years, to believe that circumstances, other people, or simple misfortune are the primary forces shaping our lives. And while those things certainly influence our experiences, they do not tell the entire story. Because within every set of circumstances, no matter how difficult, a person still retains something powerful: the ability to choose how they respond.

That choice is where responsibility lives.

Responsibility is often misunderstood. Many people associate it with burden - something heavy that limits freedom and demands constant effort. But in reality, responsibility is one of the greatest sources of freedom available to a person. The moment someone accepts genuine ownership of their choices, their habits, and their direction, they also gain the ability to change all three. And that ability is something no outside circumstance can take away.

People who carry the habit of blame often feel stuck, not because their circumstances are necessarily worse than others, but because blame removes their sense of agency. When everything is someone else's fault, there is nothing left for a person to do but wait. And waiting rarely improves anything.

In contrast, people who take ownership - even in situations that were not entirely their fault - tend to find a way forward. They ask different questions. Instead of wondering why something happened to them, they ask what they can do about it. That shift in questioning leads to a shift in action, and action is where life begins to change.

Taking responsibility does not mean pretending life is always fair. It does not mean carrying blame for things that were genuinely outside your control. What it means is recognizing that your response, your effort, and your next decision always belong to you - regardless of what came before. And once a person truly understands that, their life begins to move in a different direction.

Lesson 11 *No one will care about your future as much as you should.*

People may support, encourage, and advise us along the way, and those contributions matter. But no one else carries the same stake in your future that you do. Waiting for others to push you toward your goals, recognize your potential, or create your opportunities often leads to disappointment. Real and lasting progress begins the moment a person decides that their future deserves their own full attention and sustained effort.

Lesson 12 *Responsibility is the foundation of personal freedom.*

Freedom is often imagined as the absence of obligation, but the opposite is frequently true. People who take genuine responsibility for their finances, their habits, and their decisions tend to gain more control over their lives over time. Responsibility creates stability, and stability creates options. The more ownership a person takes, the more freedom they gradually earn.

Lesson 13 *Blaming others keeps you stuck in the same place.*

Blame can feel satisfying in the moment, especially when circumstances feel genuinely unfair. But focusing on who or what is at fault rarely changes the situation. It simply redirects energy away from solutions and toward frustration. The time and attention spent assigning blame could almost always be used more powerfully to find a new direction forward.

Lesson 14 *Your life begins to change when you stop waiting for rescue.*

Many people spend years hoping that someone or something will appear to improve their circumstances — the right person, the right opportunity, the right moment. While help from others can certainly be valuable, meaningful and lasting change almost always begins when a person decides to act on their own behalf instead of waiting for conditions to improve on their own.

Lesson 15 *Ownership creates momentum.*

The moment a person accepts full ownership of their circumstances, something shifts. Instead of focusing on what went wrong or who is at fault, they begin looking for what can be done. That shift from frustration to action generates momentum that tends to build on itself. Small steps taken from a place of ownership often lead to progress that waiting never could.

Lesson 16 *The standards you set for yourself determine the life you live.*

Every person operates according to standards they accept for themselves, whether consciously chosen or quietly inherited. These standards shape the way they work, the way they treat others, the effort they invest, and the results they expect. Raising those standards, even slightly, often produces noticeable improvement over time. What we tolerate in ourselves tends to become what we live with.

Lesson 17 *Accountability accelerates growth.*

People who hold themselves genuinely accountable for their actions tend to learn faster from their mistakes. Rather than ignoring errors or finding reasons to excuse them, they use those moments as honest information that guides better decisions going forward. Accountability is not about self-criticism — it is about the willingness to look clearly at results and ask what could be done differently.

Lesson 18 *Complaining is not a strategy.*

Expressing frustration occasionally is a natural human response. But complaining as a habit rarely produces any meaningful change. It reinforces a focus on what is wrong rather than what can be done. Solutions almost always emerge when attention shifts away from the problem itself and toward the question of what action is still available.

Lesson 19 *The direction of your life reflects the decisions you repeat.*
Occasional good decisions help, but it is the decisions we make consistently that shape long-term outcomes. How we spend our time each day, how we handle our finances, how we respond to difficulty, and how we treat the people around us - these repeated choices gradually accumulate into the life we are living. No single decision builds or breaks a life. Patterns do.

Lesson 20 *The moment you take responsibility, you take control.*

Responsibility does not guarantee that every outcome will go as planned. Life is far too unpredictable for that. But responsibility always increases a person's ability to influence their direction. When someone accepts that their actions, habits, and decisions genuinely matter, they gain something no one can give them from the outside - the power to move their own life forward.

Reflection Questions:

1. Is there an area of your life where you have been waiting for someone or something outside of yourself to create change? What would it look like to take full ownership of that area starting now?

2. What standard have you been accepting for yourself that, if you raised it, could meaningfully improve the direction you are heading?

3

Time and Direction

Of all the resources available to a person, time is the only one that cannot be replaced.

Money can be earned again. Relationships can be rebuilt. Opportunities, in many forms, tend to return. But a day that has passed is gone permanently, regardless of how it was spent or what might have been done differently. Time moves in one direction, at one speed, without exception. Yet despite this, time is often the resource people treat most carelessly.

In the early part of life, this is understandable. When the future feels wide open and consequences seem distant, it is easy to assume that there is always more time available than there actually is. Decisions feel reversible. Habits feel temporary. The idea that today's choices are quietly constructing tomorrow's circumstances does not yet feel urgent or real. What many people eventually discover is that time does not wait for awareness to catch up. It moves forward steadily, and it magnifies whatever patterns it finds along the way. A habit repeated over many years becomes deeply embedded. A skill developed consistently over time becomes a genuine strength. A responsibility repeatedly postponed becomes a problem that is far more difficult to address later. Time does not judge these patterns - it simply amplifies them.

This is why direction matters so much. Because time without direction is simply motion. It may feel like progress, but without intention guiding it, it often leads somewhere different than where a person hoped to end up. The encouraging truth is that direction can be adjusted at any point. A person who begins moving with greater intention today will experience different results one year from now than someone who continues drifting. The gap may seem small at first, but over many years it becomes significant.

Time is always working. The only question worth asking is whether it is working for you or simply passing by.

Lesson 21 *Time is always moving, whether you are moving with it or not.*

Every person receives the same twenty-four hours each day, yet those hours lead to dramatically different outcomes depending on how they are used. Some people invest their time in building skills, strengthening relationships, and creating opportunity. Others allow time to pass without much intention at all. The difference may not feel significant in a single day, but across many years it can produce results that are difficult to imagine from the starting point.

Lesson 22 *The habits you repeat eventually introduce you to your future.*

Habits often feel small and unremarkable while we are forming them. Their long-term influence, however, is enormous. A habit repeated daily becomes a pattern, a pattern becomes a lifestyle, and a lifestyle becomes an identity. When people look back at their lives, they frequently realize that their habits were quietly building their future long before they paid close enough attention to notice.

Lesson 23 *A few focused years can change the direction of a lifetime.*

Many people assume that meaningful success requires extraordinary talent, rare opportunity, or a fortunate set of circumstances. In reality, focused effort sustained consistently over several years can produce remarkable transformation. When someone commits to genuine improvement over a meaningful period of time, the results often extend far beyond what they initially believed was possible for them.

Lesson 24 *Procrastination quietly steals opportunity.*

Delaying important decisions may feel harmless or even reasonable in the moment, but postponement carries hidden costs that are easy to underestimate. Opportunities do not always remain available indefinitely. Relationships do not always stay open. Windows that exist today may be significantly smaller or closed entirely tomorrow. When people repeatedly delay action, they sometimes discover that the circumstances they were waiting for have already moved on without them.

Lesson 25 *The earlier you start building good habits, the easier life becomes.*

Habits formed early grow alongside a person's life, requiring less effort to maintain because they become part of the natural rhythm of daily living. Waiting until later to build discipline, financial awareness, or meaningful personal routines often makes those changes more difficult, because existing patterns must first be recognized, challenged, and gradually replaced. Starting early is not a guarantee of success, but it is one of the most significant advantages a person can give themselves.

Lesson 26 *Small improvements compound into powerful change.*

Improving by even a modest amount each day may seem almost too small to matter, but those improvements accumulate in ways that eventually become impossible to ignore. Just as financial investments grow through the power of compounding interest, personal growth multiplies when steady effort is applied consistently over time. The results may appear slow at first, but their eventual impact often surprises even the person who created them.

Lesson 27 *The future is built in ordinary days.*

People sometimes wait for dramatic moments or significant milestones to begin transforming their lives. But most meaningful progress happens quietly, during ordinary days that do not feel particularly important while they are happening. The decisions made in those unremarkable moments - how we spend an evening, how we handle a frustration, how seriously we take a small responsibility - are the very decisions that gradually construct the future.

Lesson 28 *Waiting for motivation often leads to waiting forever.*

Motivation is unpredictable by nature. Some days it appears naturally and powerfully, while other days it is entirely absent regardless of effort or intention. People who rely entirely on motivation to drive their progress often find themselves stalled during the inevitable periods when that motivation fades. Those who build consistent routines and habits tend to continue moving forward even when inspiration is nowhere to be found, because their progress no longer depends on how they feel on any given day.

Lesson 29 *Your future self will live with the results of today's choices.*

Every decision made today becomes part of the environment your future self will inherit. The habits formed now will either support or limit the person you are becoming. When people begin thinking about their future self not as a distant stranger but as someone they are directly responsible for, they often begin making wiser, more considered decisions in the present. The choices feel different when you understand clearly who will be living with their consequences.

Lesson 30 *Time rewards consistency more than intensity.*

Short bursts of intense effort can produce temporary results, but long-term progress almost always comes from steady, repeated action maintained over time. Consistency allows improvements to accumulate gradually, building on one another in ways that occasional intense effort cannot replicate. Many people underestimate this principle early in life, only to discover later that the most remarkable outcomes they know of were built not through dramatic effort but through quiet, reliable persistence.

Reflection Questions:

1. When you look honestly at how you spend most of your days, does your use of time reflect the future you say you want to build? If not, what is one specific change you could make this week?

2. Is there something meaningful you have been postponing, telling yourself you will get to it later? What has that delay already cost you, and what might it continue to cost if nothing changes?

4

Money and Stability

Money is one of those subjects that most people learn about the hard way.

Not because the principles are complicated. In fact, the core ideas behind financial stability are surprisingly straightforward. But because for many people, no one ever sat down and explained those principles clearly before life began demanding they already understood them. So instead of learning about money intentionally, most people learn about it through experience - through the stress of an unexpected expense, the slow weight of accumulating debt, or the quiet regret of realizing too late how much earlier decisions are still shaping current circumstances.

The result is that financial wisdom often arrives after financial mistakes have already been made.

This is more common than most people realize. Regardless of income level, background, or education, a surprising number of people move through significant portions of their lives without a clear understanding of how money actually behaves over time.

They know how to earn it. They know how to spend it. But the deeper patterns - how money grows when managed wisely, how quietly it disappears when handled carelessly, and how powerfully early habits compound into long-term outcomes - these are lessons many people discover only after wishing they had understood them sooner.

The truth about money is that it responds to behavior more than circumstance.

A person with a modest income who spends less than they earn, saves consistently, and avoids unnecessary debt will almost always build greater stability over time than someone with a high income who ignores those same principles. This is not a popular idea, because it places responsibility squarely on habits rather than on circumstances. But it is a truth that holds up consistently across a wide range of financial situations.

Money does not reward wishful thinking. It does not respond to good intentions alone. It responds to patterns - the patterns of how it is earned, how it is spent, how it is saved, and how it is allowed to work over time. Understanding those patterns does not require becoming a financial expert. It simply requires awareness, honesty, and the willingness to build habits that serve the future rather than only the present moment.

Because the decisions made around money today are quietly shaping the options available tomorrow. And for many people, that realization arrives exactly when they wish it had come much sooner.

Lesson 31 *If you do not manage money, money will eventually manage you.*

Money has a way of influencing every area of life when it is not handled with intention. Financial pressure limits choices, creates persistent stress, and forces people into decisions they would otherwise never consider. Learning to manage money thoughtfully -

before circumstances demand it - allows a person to make decisions from a position of stability rather than desperation. The difference between those two positions is significant in ways that extend far beyond finances alone.

Lesson 32 *Your spending habits matter more than your income.*

Many people believe that earning more money will automatically solve their financial difficulties. While higher income certainly creates more opportunity, the real determining factor is almost always behavior. A person who consistently spends everything they earn will feel financial pressure at any income level. The habit of spending less than you earn is simple in concept but transformative in practice, and it is available to nearly everyone regardless of how much they currently make.

Lesson 33 *Wealth grows quietly through consistency.*

Most meaningful financial growth happens slowly and without drama. Small amounts saved and invested regularly, maintained over many years, can grow into resources that once seemed far out of reach. The power of consistency in building financial stability is frequently underestimated, particularly early in life when the results feel distant. Yet it is exactly this kind of quiet, patient consistency that separates people who build genuine security from those who spend their lives feeling one unexpected expense away from difficulty.

Lesson 34 *Debt can quietly control your future.*

Borrowing money is sometimes necessary and can be managed responsibly. But unmanaged debt has a way of making decisions on a person's behalf long after the original purchase has been forgotten. Payments that seemed manageable at the beginning gradually limit the ability to save, invest, or pursue new opportunities. The true cost of debt is not just financial - it is the narrowing of future options that happens so slowly most people do not notice until the narrowing has already become significant.

Lesson 35 *If you are not making your money work, you are working harder than necessary.*

Money that sits idle rarely grows in meaningful ways. Investments - whether in financial instruments, in skills, or in opportunities - allow money to produce additional value over time alongside the effort a person is already putting in. People who understand this principle early gain a quiet advantage, because their money begins contributing to their future even during the hours when they are not actively working.

Lesson 36 *Financial ignorance is one of the most expensive conditions a person can live with.*

Mistakes involving money often carry consequences that extend for years. Without understanding how interest accumulates, how debt compounds, or how investments grow, people can unknowingly make decisions that cost them enormous amounts of time and financial progress. The good news is that this kind of ignorance is entirely correctable. Choosing to understand how money works is itself one of the most valuable financial decisions a person can make.

Lesson 37 *Lifestyle expansion can quietly trap your income.*

As income increases, the natural tendency is to increase spending alongside it. Some improvements in lifestyle are reasonable and deserved. But when every increase in income is immediately absorbed by an increase in expenses, the opportunity to build genuine financial security disappears regardless of how much is being earned. The gap between what a person earns and what they spend is where financial freedom is either created or prevented.

Lesson 38 *An emergency fund is not a luxury - it is a foundation.*

Unexpected expenses are not possibilities to plan for - they are certainties. Medical situations, vehicle repairs, job disruptions, and household emergencies will appear at some point in nearly every person's life. Without financial preparation, those moments quickly become crises that force difficult decisions under pressure. An emergency fund does not need to be large to be powerful. Even a modest reserve creates a buffer of stability that changes how a person is able to respond when life does not go according to plan.

Lesson 39 *Saving money is far easier than recovering from financial mistakes.*

Correcting significant financial problems later in life often requires years of sacrifice, discipline, and effort that could have been avoided with earlier habits. Developing responsible financial patterns early - before they feel urgent - prevents many of those problems from appearing in the first place. Prevention is rarely exciting, but the freedom it creates over time is one of the most valuable things a person can build for themselves.

Lesson 40 *Financial clarity begins with honest awareness.*

The first and most important step toward improving financial stability is simply understanding where money is actually going. Many people have only a vague sense of their spending, saving, and financial priorities. When someone begins paying genuine attention to those patterns - without judgment, but with honesty - they almost always discover opportunities for improvement they had not previously recognized. Clarity does not solve every financial problem, but nothing improves meaningfully until that clarity exists.

Reflection Questions:

1. If you examined your spending honestly over the past three

months, would your financial habits reflect the future you are hoping to build? What is one pattern you would want to change?

2. Is there a financial decision you have been avoiding or postponing - whether it involves saving, debt, or investing — that deserves your honest attention right now?

5

Courage and Fear

Fear is not the opposite of a good life. It is simply part of one.

Every person who has ever attempted something meaningful has encountered fear along the way. The person who started the business, had the honest conversation, pursued the unfamiliar opportunity, or chose to begin again after a significant loss - none of them did so without feeling some version of doubt, hesitation, or uncertainty. Fear does not disappear when a person becomes more capable or more experienced. It simply changes shape, appearing at each new threshold a person is willing to approach.

This is an important distinction, because many people spend years waiting to feel ready before they are willing to move forward. They believe that confidence must arrive before action can begin, that fear is a signal to stop rather than a natural companion to growth, and that the people who seem to move through life with ease must somehow not experience the same doubts that everyone else does.

In reality, the difference between people who make meaningful progress and those who remain stuck is rarely the absence of fear.

It is the decision about what to do with it.

Fear has a particular way of distorting perspective. It magnifies the consequences of action while minimizing the consequences of inaction. It encourages a person to imagine in vivid detail everything that could go wrong if they try, while rarely reminding them of what is quietly being lost by never trying at all. And what is lost by never trying is often far more significant than what would have been lost by attempting and falling short.

Regret, for most people, does not come from the chances they took and lost. It comes from the chances they never gave themselves. Courage is not the elimination of fear. It is the decision to move forward in spite of it. And like every meaningful skill, courage develops through practice. Each time a person acts despite uncertainty, their confidence expands slightly. Over time, those small acts of courage accumulate into a life shaped more by intention than by avoidance.

The uncomfortable truth is that a comfortable life and a meaningful life are not always the same thing. Growth lives just beyond the edge of what currently feels safe.And it is only by moving toward that edge, repeatedly and despite the fear that accompanies it, that a person discovers what they are truly capable of.

Lesson 41 *Fear of rejection blocks more opportunities than lack of ability.*

Many people assume they need more talent, more preparation, or more experience before pursuing their goals. In reality, the larger obstacle is almost always the fear of being judged, turned away, or seen as inadequate. This fear prevents people from even attempting opportunities that could genuinely change the direction of their lives. Ability can be developed over time. But the willingness to step forward despite the possibility of rejection is a choice that must be made first.

Lesson 42 *Confidence is built through action, not through waiting.*

People often believe that confidence must appear before they can begin something difficult or unfamiliar. More often, confidence develops after action has already started. Each step forward creates experience, and experience gradually replaces uncertainty with a quieter sense of capability. Waiting to feel confident before beginning is one of the most common ways people prevent themselves from ever developing the confidence they are waiting for.

Lesson 43 *Courage usually feels uncomfortable while it is happening.*

Acts of courage rarely feel dramatic or heroic in the moment. More often they feel uncertain, awkward, and genuinely intimidating. The discomfort is real. But so is the growth that follows. Some of the most important decisions a person ever makes will not feel significant until long after they are made. Learning to act despite discomfort rather than waiting until it passes is one of the most valuable things a person can develop.

Lesson 44 *Most fears shrink considerably once you face them directly.*

Fear tends to grow largest when it exists only in imagination. The mind is remarkably capable of constructing worst-case scenarios that feel vivid and convincing, making the feared situation appear far more threatening than it actually is. Once a person faces the situation directly, they frequently discover that the challenge was more manageable than expected, that the consequences of failure were more survivable than feared, and that the weight they had been carrying was heavier than it needed to be.

Lesson 45 *Rejection is temporary. Regret tends to last much longer.*

Being told no is discouraging, and that feeling is real. But rejection fades. Most people find that within days, weeks, or months, the sting of a rejection has softened considerably. Regret, however, often lingers in an entirely different way. The memory of never having tried — of allowing fear to make the decision — can remain long after the original opportunity has passed. Given the choice between risking rejection and guaranteeing regret, rejection is almost always the wiser risk.

Lesson 46 *Risk is often the price of meaningful opportunity.*

The experiences that most improve a person's life — new careers, new relationships, creative pursuits, personal reinvention — almost always require stepping into situations where the outcome is not guaranteed. Avoiding all risk rarely protects a person from difficulty. More often, it simply ensures that certain kinds of growth never happen. A life built entirely around avoiding discomfort tends to become smaller over time, not safer.

Lesson 47 *Waiting until you feel completely ready may mean waiting forever.*

Very few people ever feel entirely prepared before taking a major step forward. There is almost always something that could be learned, practiced, or improved before beginning. But the feeling of readiness does not usually precede action — it follows it. Progress almost always begins before a person feels fully equipped for it, because it is the action itself that closes the gap between where someone is and where they need to be.

Lesson 48 *Action weakens fear faster than thinking ever will.*

The more time a person spends analyzing a fear without taking any action, the stronger that fear typically becomes. Avoidance reinforces the idea that the feared thing is genuinely dangerous or beyond reach. Taking even a small step forward disrupts that cycle. It provides evidence that movement is possible, that the fear was survivable, and that the next step is closer than it appeared. Action does not eliminate fear, but it consistently reduces it in ways that thinking alone cannot.

Lesson 49 *Comfort can quietly become the ceiling of your potential.*

Remaining within familiar environments feels safe, and that safety is not without value. But comfort rarely encourages growth. Skills do not develop without challenge. Perspectives do not expand without new experiences. Opportunities do not appear without movement toward them. A person who consistently chooses comfort over growth may eventually find that their world has become smaller than they intended, not through any dramatic failure but simply through the accumulation of small, comfortable choices.

Lesson 50 *Every courageous decision expands what becomes possible for you.*

Each time a person chooses to act despite fear, something shifts. Not only does the immediate situation change, but so does the person's understanding of what they are capable of. New possibilities appear that were not visible before the step was taken. These moments may seem small individually, but over the course of a lifetime they accumulate into an entirely different kind of life - one shaped by willingness rather than avoidance, and by growth rather than the fear of it.

Reflection Questions:

1. Is there an opportunity, conversation, or decision you have been avoiding because of fear? What is the most honest cost of continuing to avoid it?

2. Think of a moment when you acted despite fear and it led to

something meaningful. What does that experience tell you about what might be waiting on the other side of the fear you are currently carrying?

6

Relationships and Influence

No person shapes their life entirely alone.

Behind every meaningful accomplishment, every period of genuine growth, and every difficult season successfully navigated, there are almost always people who played a role. Some offered encouragement at the right moment. Some provided honest feedback when it was needed most. Some simply stayed present during the times when presence itself was the most valuable thing anyone could offer.

Relationships are among the most powerful forces shaping a person's life, yet they are also among the most underestimated. People tend to think of their choices - their habits, their decisions, their effort - as the primary drivers of their outcomes. And those things matter enormously. But the people we surround ourselves with quietly influence all of them. They shape what we believe is possible, what we accept as normal, how we think about ambition and responsibility, and how we see ourselves when our own perspective becomes clouded.

This influence rarely announces itself. It works gradually, through repeated conversations, shared attitudes, and the subtle expectations that exist within every relationship. Over time, a person begins to reflect the environment they spend the most time in - not because they are weak or impressionable, but because human beings are deeply social by nature. We are shaped by one another in ways that go far deeper than most people consciously recognize.

This is why the people closest to us deserve more careful consideration than they are often given.

It is not about judging others or approaching relationships with suspicion. It is about understanding that influence is real, that environment matters, and that the people who have consistent access to our time and attention are also having consistent access to our thinking, our standards, and our sense of what is achievable.

Healthy relationships create space for growth. They offer honest encouragement, genuine challenge, and the kind of support that makes difficult periods more navigable. They remind us of our potential when we have temporarily lost sight of it, and they hold us accountable without diminishing our dignity.

Not every relationship carries those qualities. Some connections, despite genuine affection on both sides, can quietly work against the direction a person is trying to move in. Recognizing this does not require bitterness or harsh judgment. It simply requires honesty - the same honesty a person would apply to any other area of their life they were trying to improve. Because in the end, the people we choose to walk beside us are among the most consequential choices we make. And the quality of those relationships often determines the quality of the journey itself.

Lesson 51 *The people around you influence more of your life than you realize.*

Human behavior is deeply shaped by environment. The attitudes, habits, expectations, and beliefs of those closest to us gradually begin to influence our own thinking and actions, often in ways we are not consciously aware of. Over time, this influence can shape our goals, our standards, and our sense of what is normal or possible. Understanding the depth of this influence is the first step toward being more intentional about the relationships we allow to become part of our daily lives.

Lesson 52 *Your closest relationships often reflect the standards you have accepted for yourself.*

The people we allow into our inner circle tend to share similar expectations about effort, responsibility, and personal behavior - not always because we chose them for that reason, but because shared standards create natural compatibility. When someone begins raising their own standards, they often find that their relationships begin to shift as well. The connections that support growth tend to strengthen, while those built on lower expectations may naturally create more friction or distance.

Lesson 53 *Not every relationship is meant to last forever, and that is not a failure.*

Some connections serve a meaningful purpose during a specific season of life. They offer companionship, support, or shared experience that is genuinely valuable at the time. As people grow, change, and develop new priorities, some of those relationships evolve naturally while others fade. Accepting this reality allows a person to appreciate past connections without guilt, and to release relationships that have run their natural course without treating the ending as a reflection of anyone's worth.

Lesson 54 *Encouraging relationships accelerate growth in ways that are difficult to achieve alone.*

Supportive people create environments where improvement feels not only possible but expected. Genuine encouragement, honest feedback, and shared ambition help individuals pursue goals they might hesitate to attempt in isolation. Being surrounded by people who believe in growth - who take their own lives seriously and expect the same from those around them - makes the work of becoming a better person feel less like a solitary struggle and more like a shared direction.

Lesson 55 *Negative environments quietly limit potential over time.*

Constant criticism, persistent pessimism, and an atmosphere of complaint or complacency can slowly erode a person's motivation, confidence, and willingness to take meaningful risks. The effect is rarely sudden or dramatic. It accumulates gradually, until one day a person realizes that their ambitions have quietly shrunk to fit the expectations of the environment they have been living in. Recognizing this pattern early makes it possible to address it before too much ground has been lost.

Lesson 56 *Boundaries are not walls - they are the architecture of healthy relationships.*

Healthy relationships require mutual respect, and mutual respect requires clarity about what each person needs and expects. Establishing honest boundaries is not about pushing people away or creating unnecessary distance. It is about creating the conditions under which a relationship can function well over time. Without boundaries, resentment tends to build quietly until it disrupts connections that might otherwise have remained strong.

Lesson 57 *True loyalty never requires the sacrifice of your self-respect.*

Loyalty is one of the most valued qualities in any relationship, and rightly so. But loyalty has limits that are worth understanding clearly. A relationship that consistently demands the compromise of personal values, dignity, or wellbeing in order to demonstrate commitment is not asking for loyalty - it is asking for something closer to surrender. Genuine loyalty is always mutual, always built on respect, and never requires a person to diminish themselves in order to prove it.

Lesson 58 *Choose relationships that make the person you want to become feel more attainable.*

The people closest to us either expand or contract our sense of what is possible. Those who believe in growth, who take their own development seriously, and who hold meaningful expectations for themselves and those around them make it easier for us to do the same. Over time, being in the consistent presence of people who are genuinely trying to improve creates an environment where growth feels like a natural direction rather than an exceptional effort.

Lesson 59 *Distance and time reveal which relationships were built on genuine care.*

Some connections feel strong largely because of shared routine, proximity, or convenience. When circumstances change - when distance increases, when life takes people in different directions, or when the familiar context disappears - the true foundation of a relationship often becomes visible. Connections built on genuine care tend to endure those changes. Those built primarily on habit or convenience often reveal their nature more clearly when the habit or convenience is no longer present.

Lesson 60 *Healthy relationships multiply your strength during the most difficult seasons.*

Life inevitably includes periods of genuine difficulty - loss, uncertainty, failure, and the kind of challenges that cannot simply be thought or worked through alone. During those seasons, the quality of a person's relationships becomes one of the most significant factors in how they are able to respond. Supportive connections provide perspective when thinking becomes narrow, encouragement when motivation fades, and the simple but powerful reminder that difficulty does not have to be faced in isolation. The investment made in healthy relationships during ordinary times pays its greatest return during extraordinary ones.

Reflection Questions:

1. When you consider the people you spend the most time with, do those relationships generally move you toward the person you want to become, or do they quietly pull in a different direction? What does your honest answer tell you?

2. Is there a relationship in your life - whether personal or professional - where the absence of clear boundaries has been creating friction, resentment, or imbalance? What would it look like to address that honestly?

7

Discipline and Personal Growth

Most people admire the results of discipline without fully understanding what discipline actually is.

They see the person who is physically strong and assume natural ability. They observe the person who has built financial security and assume fortunate circumstances. They notice the person who has mastered a skill, built something meaningful, or sustained progress through difficult periods - and they often attribute those outcomes to some quality that person was simply born with or lucky enough to encounter.

What tends to remain invisible is the quiet, unglamorous work that produced those results.

Discipline is not a personality trait reserved for exceptional people. It is not the absence of doubt, the elimination of distraction, or the ability to feel motivated every single day. Discipline is far simpler and far more available than most people realize. It is the decision to show up consistently - not perfectly, not dramatically, but reliably - in the direction of something that matters.

That decision, repeated over time, produces results that nothing else can replicate.

The reason discipline is often misunderstood is that it is invisible at the beginning. The early stages of any disciplined effort rarely look impressive. The person waking up early to read, the person setting aside a small amount of money each week, the person practicing a skill in private long before anyone notices - none of these moments appear significant while they are happening. They feel ordinary, and sometimes even pointless, because the results they are building are not yet visible.

But invisible does not mean absent. Those efforts are accumulating beneath the surface, compounding quietly, building a foundation that will eventually support outcomes the early effort made possible.

This is the fundamental nature of personal growth. It does not announce itself. It does not unfold on a visible schedule. It develops through the steady repetition of effort that most people are unwilling to sustain long enough to see the results. Discipline also changes a person's relationship with difficulty. When someone has built the habit of doing hard things consistently, individual challenges begin to feel less threatening. Not because the challenges become easier, but because the person has developed evidence - accumulated through their own experience - that difficulty can be moved through. That evidence becomes one of the most valuable things a person can carry.

Growth is not a destination. It is a direction.

And discipline is simply the commitment to keep moving in that direction, regardless of how the day feels, how far the goal seems, or how long the process appears to be taking. The people who build the lives they most want are rarely the most talented or the most fortunate. They are most often the ones who decided, at some point, that consistency was more valuable than comfort. And then they proved it, one ordinary day at a time.

Lesson 61 *Discipline creates the freedom most people spend their lives searching for.*

At first glance, discipline can appear restrictive. It requires effort, consistency, and the willingness to prioritize long-term results over short-term comfort. But the freedom that disciplined habits eventually produce is extraordinary. Financial discipline creates independence. Health discipline creates vitality and energy. Personal discipline creates control over time, attention, and opportunity. The temporary discomfort of building discipline is one of the most worthwhile investments a person can make in their own future.

Lesson 62 *Motivation is unreliable. Habits are dependable.*

Motivation is a feeling, and like all feelings it is subject to change without warning. Some days it arrives naturally and powerfully. Other days it is entirely absent regardless of how much a person wants to move forward. People who rely on motivation as their primary driver of progress will always be at the mercy of how they feel on a given day. People who build genuine habits create a system that continues functioning even when motivation has temporarily disappeared, because the behavior no longer depends on the feeling.

Lesson 63 *Small actions repeated consistently create results that occasional large efforts cannot.*

Many people underestimate the impact of small, repeated efforts because the changes they produce are gradual rather than dramatic. A single session of reading, exercising, saving, or practicing a skill may seem almost insignificant. But when that action is repeated daily, weekly, and monthly over the course of years, it accumulates into something that cannot be achieved any other way. Consistency is not a shortcut - it is simply the most reliable path to results that actually last.

Lesson 64 *Easy choices repeated over time often create difficult futures.*

Choosing convenience over effort, comfort over discipline, or avoidance over responsibility may feel reasonable in any individual moment. The problem is that these choices do not exist in isolation. They compound, just as good habits do, gradually shaping circumstances that become harder to navigate the longer they continue. The person who consistently chooses ease today is often the same person who faces significantly harder challenges tomorrow - not as punishment, but as the natural consequence of accumulated choices.

Lesson 65 *Difficult choices made consistently tend to create easier, more stable futures.*

Investing effort early - learning new skills, building financial discipline, maintaining health, and making responsible decisions before they become urgent - may feel challenging in the beginning. These choices require something in the present in exchange for something better in the future. But that exchange is almost always worth making. The person who consistently makes the harder choice today is quietly building a future that requires far less crisis management, far less recovery, and far more genuine freedom.

Lesson 66 *Consistency matters more than intensity.*

Intense periods of effort can produce impressive short-term results, but they are difficult to sustain and rarely create the deep, durable progress that consistent effort produces. Showing up regularly - even with modest effort, even on days when the results feel invisible - builds something that occasional intensity cannot. The person who works steadily and reliably over many years will almost always outperform the person who works intensely for short bursts followed by long periods of inactivity.

Lesson 67 *Your daily routine is quietly constructing the life you will be living in five years.*

The way a person spends their ordinary days is not separate from the life they are building - it is the life they are building. Routines influence productivity, health, learning, relationships, and financial stability in ways that accumulate steadily over time. Most people do not design their daily routines consciously, which means those routines are often shaped by habit, convenience, and circumstance rather than by intention. Examining and adjusting those routines is one of the most direct ways to change the direction of a person's future.

Lesson 68 *Growth often feels uncomfortable while it is happening, and that discomfort is a sign it is real.*

Learning new skills, changing deeply held habits, and pushing beyond familiar limits frequently involves frustration, uncertainty, and the uncomfortable feeling of not yet being good at something. These experiences can feel discouraging, particularly when progress seems slow or invisible. But discomfort during growth is not a warning sign - it is evidence that real development is taking place. The absence of discomfort during a period of intended growth is often a sign that the effort is not yet reaching far enough.

Lesson 69 *The strongest people build themselves slowly, through patience and repeated effort.*

Personal strength - whether physical, emotional, financial, or intellectual - is rarely the result of dramatic transformation. It develops gradually, through the patient accumulation of effort over time. Each challenge navigated, each skill developed, and each habit strengthened adds another layer of capability that the previous version of the person did not possess. The most capable people are usually not the ones who started with the most - they are the ones who kept building, quietly and consistently, long after others had stopped.

Lesson 70 *Progress belongs to those who keep going when results are not yet visible.*

One of the most common reasons people abandon meaningful efforts is that progress during the early and middle stages is often invisible or disappointingly slow. The results exist - they are accumulating beneath the surface - but they have not yet reached the threshold where they become undeniable. The people who eventually experience the most significant outcomes are frequently not the most talented. They are simply the ones who continued showing up during the long, unremarkable stretches when quitting would have been easy and understandable.

Reflection Questions:

1. Is there an area of your life where you have been relying on motivation rather than building a consistent habit? What would it look like to show up in that area regardless of how you feel on a given day?

2. When you look at your daily routine honestly, does it reflect the life you want to be living in five years? If not, what is one specific adjustment you could begin making this week?

8

Perspective and Wisdom

There is a kind of understanding that cannot be rushed.

It does not come from reading the right books, receiving the right advice, or being told the correct answer at the right moment. It develops slowly, through the accumulation of experience - through mistakes made and examined, through challenges navigated and reflected upon, through expectations that reality did not meet and the gradual adjustment that followed. It is the kind of understanding that changes not just what a person knows, but how they see.

That understanding is perspective. And its deeper form, earned over time, is wisdom.

Perspective is one of the quietest gifts that experience offers. The situation that once felt catastrophic begins to look manageable with distance. The failure that once felt permanent begins to reveal the lesson it was carrying. The comparison that once felt urgent begins to lose its power when a person becomes more interested in their own direction than in measuring themselves against someone else's.

None of these shifts happen all at once. They arrive gradually, almost imperceptibly, until one day a person realizes they are responding to life differently than they once did.

This gradual shift is not accidental. It is the product of reflection. Experience alone does not produce wisdom. Many people accumulate decades of experience without ever extracting the understanding those experiences were capable of offering. What transforms experience into wisdom is the willingness to pause, to examine honestly what happened and why, and to carry those insights forward into future decisions. Without that reflection, experience simply becomes history. With it, experience becomes one of the most powerful teachers available.

Perspective also changes the way a person relates to difficulty. Early in life, setbacks often feel final - as though a failure in one area defines the whole of what is possible. With time, most people begin to see that failure is rarely the endpoint it appeared to be. It is more often a redirection, a source of information, or simply the necessary cost of attempting something that mattered. The people who develop this perspective do not become indifferent to difficulty. They simply stop allowing difficulty to have the final word.

Perhaps the most valuable shift that perspective brings is a quieter relationship with comparison. In earlier years, it is natural to measure progress against the visible lives of others - their achievements, their possessions, their apparent confidence and ease. But with experience comes the recognition that outward appearances reveal very little about the actual texture of someone's life. Every person is navigating their own challenges, their own doubts, and their own private struggles. Understanding this does not eliminate ambition. It simply frees a person to pursue their own direction without the unnecessary weight of measuring it constantly against someone else's.

Wisdom, in the end, is not a destination. It is not a state of having finally figured everything out. It is the ongoing willingness to learn, to adjust, and to see more clearly with each passing year.
And the remarkable thing about that kind of seeing is that it never stops deepening.

Lesson 71 *Comparison often obscures the progress you have already made.*

When a person consistently measures their life against the visible achievements of others, they tend to overlook the genuine progress they have made along their own path. Progress becomes difficult to recognize when attention is focused entirely on someone else's position rather than on the distance between where you started and where you currently stand. Your journey has its own timeline, its own challenges, and its own form of progress - and comparison rarely does justice to any of those things.

Lesson 72 *Most people are still figuring life out, regardless of how certain they appear.*

It is easy to assume, particularly when looking at the lives of others from the outside, that most people have things more figured out than you do. In reality, nearly everyone is navigating uncertainty, adjusting their direction, learning through experience, and carrying questions they have not yet answered. The confidence that others project is frequently a presentation rather than a complete picture. Understanding this makes it easier to extend both patience and compassion - to others and to yourself.

Lesson 73 *Failure often teaches faster and more thoroughly than success.*
Success, while deeply valuable, has a way of concealing weaknesses. When things go well, there is little pressure to examine why, and the lessons embedded in the experience often go unnoticed. Failure, by contrast, demands examination. It forces a person to confront what went wrong, what they assumed incorrectly, and what they might do differently. This process of honest reflection, though uncomfortable,

frequently produces insights that become the foundation of stronger decisions going forward.

Lesson 74 *Your mindset determines your experience of the same circumstances.*

Two people can encounter identical situations and emerge with entirely different experiences based on the perspective they brought to it. One person sees an obstacle; another sees a problem worth solving. One person sees a setback; another sees information. The circumstances themselves do not change - but the meaning assigned to them, and the response that meaning produces, can lead to dramatically different outcomes. Developing awareness of how you interpret your circumstances is one of the most practical forms of personal growth available.

Lesson 75 *Gratitude improves the quality of ordinary life without requiring circumstances to change.*

When a person's attention is focused primarily on what is missing, satisfaction remains perpetually out of reach because there will always be something not yet achieved, not yet acquired, or not yet resolved. Gratitude shifts that focus without requiring any change in external circumstances. It directs attention toward what is already present - relationships, health, small pleasures, progress already made - and in doing so, it changes the actual experience of daily life in ways that waiting for better circumstances rarely does.

Lesson 76 *Everyone's timeline is different, and comparing yours to someone else's is rarely useful.*

Life does not unfold according to a universal schedule. Some people find their direction early; others discover it after years of searching. Some build stability quickly; others do so after significant struggle and redirection. Comparing your timeline to someone else's creates pressure that is almost entirely unproductive, because it measures your progress against a standard that has nothing to do with your actual starting point, circumstances, or path. The only timeline worth measuring yourself against is your own.

Lesson 77 *Perfection is not required for progress, and waiting for it guarantees neither.*

Many people delay beginning something meaningful because they believe they must do it correctly, completely, or impressively from the start. In reality, meaningful progress almost always begins through imperfect attempts that gradually improve through repetition and experience. The willingness to begin imperfectly is not a compromise - it is the actual mechanism through which competence develops. Perfection, as a prerequisite for starting, is one of the most reliable ways to ensure that nothing gets started at all.

Lesson 78 *Life becomes considerably lighter when you stop struggling against what you cannot control.*

Every person's life contains circumstances that lie genuinely beyond their ability to influence. Fighting those circumstances - spending energy on frustration, resistance, or the wish that things were different - rarely changes them and almost always creates unnecessary suffering in the process. Learning to direct attention and effort toward what can actually be controlled - attitude, effort, response, and decision - not only reduces stress but creates the mental clarity needed to act more effectively within whatever circumstances actually exist.

Lesson 79 *Patience is not passive waiting - it is the active commitment to continue during uncertainty.*

Many worthwhile goals require more time than initial enthusiasm anticipates. The period between beginning and arriving is often longer, quieter, and more uncertain than expected. Patience is the quality that allows a person to remain committed during that period

- not because they are indifferent to results, but because they understand that meaningful outcomes rarely arrive on the timeline urgency would prefer. Developing patience is not about lowering expectations. It is about trusting the process long enough for the process to produce something real.

Lesson 80 *Wisdom grows not from experience alone, but from the honest reflection that follows it.*

A person can live through decades of experience and extract very little wisdom from them if those experiences are never examined honestly. What transforms experience into genuine understanding is the willingness to pause, to ask what actually happened and why, to acknowledge what was done well and what might have been done differently, and to carry those insights consciously into what comes next. This kind of reflection does not require perfection or harsh self-judgment. It simply requires honesty and the genuine desire to learn.

Reflection Questions:

1. Is there a past failure or disappointment you have not yet fully examined for what it was trying to teach you? What honest insight might still be available from that experience if you were willing to look at it clearly?

2. In what area of your life have you been comparing your progress or timeline to someone else's in a way that is creating unnecessary pressure? What would change if you released that comparison and focused entirely on your own direction?

9

Reinvention and Change

One of the most quietly liberating truths about life is that it is never fully finished shaping itself.

No matter how much time has passed, no matter how fixed a person's circumstances may appear, and no matter how long a particular path has been followed, the possibility of change remains available. Not as a distant hope or an unrealistic fantasy, but as a genuine and practical reality that countless people have discovered at every stage of life, often long after they believed their direction was permanently set.

Reinvention is not a dramatic event reserved for extraordinary people in extraordinary circumstances. It is simply the recognition that growth does not stop at a predetermined point, that people are capable of more than their history suggests, and that a different future does not require a perfect past.

For many people, the impulse toward reinvention arrives during a period of honest reflection. They look at the life they are living and recognize that it no longer fully reflects the person they have become. Priorities have shifted. Values have deepened. The things that once seemed most important have quietly given way to something that feels more true. And in that recognition, a question begins to form - not a desperate question, but a genuinely curious one. What would it look like to begin moving in a different direction?

That question is the beginning of reinvention.

What often holds people back is not the absence of desire or ability. It is the weight of accumulated identity. We become attached to who we have been, to the roles we have occupied, and to the expectations - our own and others' - that have built up around us over time. Stepping away from those familiar structures requires a particular kind of courage, not because the new direction is necessarily dangerous, but because it is unknown. And the unknown, regardless of how much better it might turn out to be, always requires something from us before it reveals itself.

Change also carries the vulnerability of beginning again. There is humility in starting something new, in being a beginner after having been established somewhere else, in not yet knowing what a more experienced version of yourself will eventually understand. That humility is not weakness. It is one of the most honest and necessary postures a person can bring to any new chapter of their life.

The experiences gathered in earlier stages are never wasted, even when the direction changes entirely. They become a foundation of perspective, resilience, and self-knowledge that younger beginners simply do not yet possess. Every previous chapter contributes something to the one that follows, even when the connection is not immediately visible.

Reinvention does not erase what came before. It builds upon it. And the moment a person decides to begin again - regardless of how late it feels, regardless of how uncertain the path appears —

that decision itself is the first proof that the next chapter is already underway.

Lesson 81 *Your past does not permanently define what your future is allowed to contain.*

While past decisions shape current circumstances, they do not determine what remains possible going forward. People have demonstrated, in every imaginable set of circumstances, the ability to learn from experience and redirect their lives in meaningful new ways. The past is context, not sentence. It informs the starting point of the next chapter without writing the content of it. What a person does with what they have learned matters far more than what they wish they had done differently.

Lesson 82 *It is rarely as late as fear suggests it is to begin something meaningful.*

Fear has a way of convincing people that windows have closed permanently, that certain opportunities belong only to the young, and that the time required to build something new is simply no longer available. In reality, meaningful accomplishments, new careers, creative pursuits, and significant personal transformations have been initiated by people at every stage of life. The belief that it is too late is almost always a feeling masquerading as a fact. Examining that belief honestly usually reveals more room for possibility than fear was willing to show.

Lesson 83 *Dissatisfaction, honestly examined, is one of the most useful signals available.*

The discomfort a person feels when their life no longer aligns with their values, priorities, or sense of purpose is not simply an inconvenience to be managed. It is information. It is the internal signal that something meaningful is asking to be addressed - that growth is being called for, that a direction needs reconsidering, or that a change long delayed has finally become impossible to ignore. People who learn to listen to that signal honestly, rather than suppressing it or distracting themselves from it, are often the ones who make the most significant and satisfying changes in their lives.

Lesson 84 *Significant transformation almost always begins with small, deliberate changes.*

The idea of complete reinvention can feel overwhelming when viewed as a single leap. But most meaningful change does not happen all at once. It begins with modest adjustments - a new habit introduced, a different perspective adopted, a small step taken in an unfamiliar direction. These initial changes are not insignificant. They are the actual mechanism through which larger transformation eventually becomes possible. The willingness to begin small is not a limitation. It is the most reliable path toward something genuinely different.

Lesson 85 *Beginning again requires humility, and humility is a strength worth developing.*

Starting something new - particularly after having established experience somewhere else - means accepting a period of not yet knowing what a more practiced version of yourself will eventually understand. That experience of being a beginner again can feel uncomfortable, particularly for people who are accustomed to competence in their existing area of life. But the willingness to be a beginner, to ask questions, to learn openly, and to move through the awkward early stages without abandoning the effort is one of the most valuable qualities a person pursuing reinvention can bring to the process.

Lesson 86 *Every experience you have gathered becomes an asset in whatever comes next.*

A change in direction does not erase what came before it. The knowledge, judgment, resilience, and self-awareness developed through previous experiences travel with a person into every new chapter they begin. Often, these qualities prove more valuable in the new direction than they were in the original one, because they are now supported by a depth of perspective that only comes from having navigated real challenges over real time. Nothing a person has genuinely learned is ever wasted, even when the path it was gathered on has been left behind.

Lesson 87 *Reinvention is not an exception to personal growth - it is an expression of it.*

Growth is not a process that arrives at a final destination and stops. It continues throughout life for as long as a person remains willing to learn, to question, and to evolve. Reinvention is simply what growth looks like when the changes required are larger than a simple adjustment. It is the natural result of a person who has developed beyond the life they were previously living and has the courage to honor that development by moving in the direction it is pointing. Far from being unusual, reinvention is one of the clearest signs that growth is genuinely alive in a person's life.

Lesson 88 *The fear of judgment loses its power the moment you decide your direction matters more.*

One of the most common forces that delays reinvention is the concern about how others will respond. What will people think? What will they say? Will they understand, or will they question the decision? These concerns are natural, but they are worth examining honestly. The people most affected by the direction of your life are not the ones watching from the outside - they are you and the people closest to you. When a person decides that their own growth and fulfillment deserve more weight than the opinions of observers, the fear of judgment tends to lose much of the influence it once held.

Lesson 89 *Curiosity is the quality that keeps growth alive at every stage of life.*

Learning does not belong exclusively to the young, and growth is not reserved for people who have not yet reached a certain age or stage of life. Curiosity - the genuine desire to understand, explore, and discover - remains available to any person who chooses to cultivate it. It is the quality that keeps a person engaged with life rather than simply moving through it. Those who remain curious tend to find new directions, new interests, and new sources of meaning long after others have stopped looking for them.

Lesson 90 *The next chapter of your life does not require permission - it requires a decision.*

Change does not usually wait for an ideal moment, a significant milestone, or the approval of the people around you. It begins when a person makes a genuine internal decision to move in a different direction and then takes the first step that decision requires. That step does not need to be large. It does not need to be perfectly planned or universally understood. It simply needs to be taken. The decision to begin is itself the beginning, and from that point forward, the next chapter is already in motion.

Reflection Questions:

1. Is there an area of your life where dissatisfaction has been present long enough that it deserves to be treated as a signal rather than simply endured? What might that signal be telling you about a change that is overdue?

2. Is there a version of your life - a direction, a pursuit, or a change - that you have been postponing because it feels too late, too uncertain, or too difficult to explain to others? What would it mean for your future if you decided to take the first step toward it anyway?

10

The Life That Remains

There comes a point in almost every person's life when the pace slows just enough to allow a clearer view of the path already traveled.

It does not always arrive at a predictable moment or a particular age. Sometimes it comes during a quiet evening when the busyness of the day has temporarily settled. Sometimes it arrives during a significant transition - a milestone reached, a chapter closed, or a relationship that has changed in ways that invite reflection. However it arrives, it brings with it a particular quality of awareness that the earlier, faster-moving years rarely permitted.

From that vantage point, things begin to look different.

Decisions that once felt routine begin to reveal the long-term weight they were carrying all along. Habits that seemed small begin to show their true cumulative influence. Relationships that were sometimes taken for granted begin to stand out as among the most genuinely valuable things a life can contain. And the things that once demanded so much attention - the comparisons, the urgencies, the anxieties about what others thought - begin to look considerably smaller than they once did.

This is not regret. Or at least, it does not have to be. It is clarity. And clarity, whenever it arrives, is one of the most useful things a person can possess - because clarity does not only illuminate the past. It also informs the future.

Because here is what reflection makes unmistakably clear: life is not finished simply because a certain amount of it has already passed. The capacity for growth does not have an expiration date. The ability to choose differently, to begin something new, to deepen a relationship, to develop a new understanding, or to live with greater intention than before - none of these belong exclusively to the young or the early. They belong to anyone who is still here and still willing.

The life that remains is not a smaller version of the life that has passed. It is simply the next portion of a continuing story - one that is still being written, still capable of surprise, and still shaped in meaningful ways by the choices made within it.

Every day that remains is still a day of genuine possibility.
Not because everything can be changed, and not because every door that has closed will reopen. But because the most important force in a person's life - the capacity to choose how they show up, what they value, how they treat others, and what they are willing to continue building - remains available for as long as life itself continues.

That is not a small thing.

That is everything.

Lesson 91 *Life rarely unfolds exactly as planned, and that is not always a loss.*

Unexpected events, unplanned detours, and circumstances that arrived without invitation are part of every person's story. Some of these disruptions lead to difficulty. But others - perhaps more than is immediately obvious - lead somewhere genuinely better than the original plan would have allowed. Flexibility and the willingness to adapt are not signs of a life that went wrong. They are often the qualities that allowed it to go somewhere more meaningful than rigid planning ever could have produced.

Lesson 92 *Your legacy is shaped far more by daily behavior than by occasional achievement.*

Large accomplishments are meaningful and worth pursuing. But the most enduring impression a person leaves on the world and on the people closest to them is rarely built through singular moments of success. It is built through the consistent texture of how they lived - how they treated people in ordinary moments, what they stood for when it was inconvenient, the patience they offered, the honesty they maintained, and the effort they invested quietly and without recognition. Daily behavior, accumulated over years, is where legacy is actually constructed.

Lesson 93 *The most valuable lessons are rarely the ones told to us - they are the ones we live through.*

Advice, instruction, and the wisdom of others can provide genuine guidance, and there is real value in seeking it. But the understanding that changes a person most deeply is almost always the understanding earned through personal experience - through attempting something and failing, through caring deeply and being disappointed, through making a decision and living with its consequences. These experiences carry a weight and specificity that secondhand knowledge rarely can. They become part of how a person sees, not just what they know.

Lesson 94 *Time has a way of clarifying what truly deserves your attention.*

As years accumulate, many of the things that once felt urgent gradually reveal themselves as less important than they appeared. Petty conflicts, minor embarrassments, and the opinions of people who were never truly invested in your wellbeing begin to lose their grip. At the same time, the things that genuinely matter - health, honest relationships, meaningful work, and the quality of attention given to ordinary moments — tend to become more visible and more precious. Time does not change what matters. It simply makes it harder to pretend that what doesn't matter does.

Lesson 95 *Regret most often comes from the opportunities never pursued, not from the attempts that fell short.*

When people reflect honestly on the sources of their deepest regrets, the pattern is remarkably consistent. It is rarely the risks taken and lost that linger most painfully. It is the risks never taken - the conversations never started, the pursuits never attempted, the changes never made - that tend to occupy the most persistent space in memory. Failure can be examined, learned from, and eventually released. But the question of what might have been, had a person simply been willing to try, has a way of remaining open far longer.

Lesson 96 *Personal growth continues for as long as a person remains willing to pursue it.*

Growth is not a process that belongs exclusively to the young or to those in the early stages of building a life. It continues for as long as a person remains curious, honest, and willing to examine their own patterns with the intention of improving them. The form that growth takes may change over time - the skills developed, the habits refined, the perspectives deepened - but the capacity for it does not diminish with age. It simply requires the ongoing decision to remain open to it.

Lesson 97 *A meaningful life is built through the accumulation of intentional choices.*

Meaning rarely arrives as a sudden gift or a single defining moment. It develops gradually, through the repeated choice to live in alignment with what genuinely matters - to invest in relationships that deserve investment, to pursue work that reflects real values, to treat people with the care and honesty they deserve, and to make decisions that the future self will be grateful for rather than burdened by. Intentional living is not a complicated philosophy. It is simply the ongoing practice of choosing on purpose rather than by default.

Lesson 98 *Kindness and integrity leave impressions that outlast almost everything else.*

Accomplishments fade in memory. Possessions lose their significance. Status shifts with circumstance. But the way a person consistently treated others - the generosity they offered without expectation, the honesty they maintained under pressure, the dignity they extended to people who had no power to reward them for it - tends to remain in the memory of those who experienced it long after almost everything else has blurred. Character, expressed through consistent behavior over time, is among the most enduring things a person can build.

Lesson 99 *The quality of your inner life shapes the quality of everything that surrounds it.*

External circumstances matter, and no honest accounting of life pretends otherwise. But the internal landscape - the way a person relates to themselves, the stories they tell about who they are and what is possible, the degree of peace or conflict they carry within - has an enormous influence on how every external circumstance is experienced. A person at genuine peace with themselves experiences the same world very differently than someone at war with it. Cultivating that inner quality is not a luxury. It is among the most practical investments a person can make.

Lesson 100 *The best moment to apply a life lesson is always the present one.*

Understanding accumulates through reading, reflection, and experience. But understanding that is never applied remains only an idea. The lessons most worth having are not the ones stored away for future reference - they are the ones brought into contact with actual decisions, real relationships, and the specific circumstances of a life being actively lived. Every moment of genuine awareness is also an invitation. The invitation is always the same: not someday, not when conditions improve, not after the right preparation. Now, with what is available, in the life that is actually here.

Reflection Questions:

1. When you consider the life you have lived so far - the choices made, the habits formed, the relationships invested in or neglected - what is the most honest and useful insight that reflection offers you about the direction you want to move in from here?

2. If you imagine yourself looking back on this specific period of your life ten years from now, what would you most want to be able to say that you did with the time and opportunity that was available to you right now?

Closing Reflection

At some point in life, almost everyone looks back and begins to see their journey more clearly than they could while they were living through it.

They begin to notice the habits they allowed to form, the decisions they made without fully understanding their weight, the opportunities they pursued, and the ones they quietly let pass. What once felt confusing begins to make sense. What once seemed random begins to reveal its patterns. And the lessons that were invisible in earlier years begin to stand out with a clarity that only distance and experience can provide.

This kind of reflection is not about criticism. It is not about cataloguing regrets or measuring a life against some imagined version of what it should have been. It is about understanding - and understanding, whenever it arrives, is always useful.
Because the same awareness that allows a person to see the past more clearly also allows them to approach the future with greater intention.

The lessons in this book are not the final word on any of the subjects they address. Life is far too specific, too varied, and too personal for any single collection of ideas to capture completely. What these lessons offer instead is a framework - a set of patterns worth recognizing, principles worth considering, and questions worth sitting with as you move through whatever chapter of life you are currently living.

Some of these ideas may have confirmed things you already sensed but had not yet put into words. Others may have introduced a perspective you had not previously considered. And perhaps a few arrived at a moment when you needed them in a way you could not have anticipated before you began reading. Whatever your experience of this book has been, the most important thing is what happens next.

Not what you now know. But what you choose to do with that knowing. Because awareness that is never applied remains only an idea. And an idea, however good, changes nothing on its own. What changes things is the decision - made in an ordinary moment, without fanfare or perfect conditions - to take what has been understood and bring it into contact with the actual life being lived.

That decision is always available.

It is available right now.

And that, in the end, is the most encouraging truth this book can offer. The life ahead of you is still being written. The habits that will shape it are still being formed. The decisions that will determine its direction are still being made. And the awareness you carry into those moments - about time, about responsibility, about courage, about the people you choose, about the standards you hold for yourself - will quietly influence all of it.

You already have more than you may realize.

Now go use it.

A Final Note from the Author

If there is one idea that runs beneath every lesson in this book, it is this:

Life is shaped gradually, by choices that rarely feel significant in the moment they are made. Not by dramatic decisions or extraordinary circumstances. Not by rare talent or perfect timing. But by the quiet accumulation of small choices, repeated over days and weeks and years, that eventually construct something undeniable - a direction, a character, a life.

How we spend our time when no one is watching. How we respond to difficulty when the outcome is uncertain. The habits we choose to build and the ones we choose to release. The people we decide to walk beside and the standards we decide to hold for ourselves. The courage we extend toward the life we actually want, rather than settling indefinitely for the one that simply feels safe. These choices do not announce their importance while they are being made. They accumulate quietly, beneath the surface of ordinary days, until one day their influence becomes impossible to ignore.

The hope behind this book is simple: that these lessons may help someone recognize those patterns a little earlier - while there is still time to use what they reveal, while the habits are still forming, while the direction is still being set, and while the life ahead still holds more chapters than the ones already written.

You do not need to have everything figured out. You do not need to begin perfectly or proceed without uncertainty. You simply need to begin - with honesty about where you are, with intention about where you want to go, and with the understanding that every step taken in the right direction, no matter how small, is a step that compounds into something greater than it first appeared.

The moment a person becomes genuinely aware of the direction they are moving is the same moment they gain the power to change it.

That moment is now.

And now is always enough to begin.

— *Noah Wayan*

A Moment for Reflection

Before you close this book, take a moment to be still.

Not to review everything you have read. Not to create a plan or set a goal or measure how far you have to go. Simply to pause - honestly and without pressure - and allow the ideas that mattered most to you to settle.

Consider the lessons that stayed with you. The ones that made you slow down. The ones that felt uncomfortably familiar, or that described something you have known quietly for longer than you have been willing to admit.

When you are ready, bring your attention to these questions. Not as an assignment, but as an honest conversation with yourself.

What habits are quietly shaping my future right now - and are they building the life I actually want?

What decision have I been postponing that I already know deserves my attention?

Where have I been waiting - for better timing, more certainty, or someone else's permission - when what was truly needed was simply my own choice to begin?

What kind of life do I want the next chapter of my story to reflect?

These questions do not require immediate answers. Some of the most valuable reflection happens slowly, over days or weeks, as the questions continue working beneath the surface of ordinary life. What matters most is that you take them seriously. Because awareness is always the first step toward meaningful change. And a single moment of genuine awareness - encountered at the right time, in the right frame of mind, and met with the honest willingness to act on what it reveals - can quietly change the entire direction of a life.

This may be that moment.

Trust it.

About the Author

Noah Wayan writes about life from the perspective of experience, reflection, and growth. His work explores the lessons people often come to understand only after time has passed-insights about choices, habits, relationships, and the quiet patterns that shape our lives.

Through thoughtful observation and clear, relatable writing, Noah encourages readers to reflect on their own journeys and recognize the lessons that can lead to a more intentional future.

If I Only Knew is a collection of those insights-simple truths many people eventually discover, shared while there is still time to use them.

Also by Noah Wayan

All Was Good Until You...is a powerful, eye-opening exploration of how emotional immaturity - hidden behind silence, control, and unhealed wounds - quietly erodes our closest relationships across every corner of life.

Can You Hear Me?...is a heartfelt call from men who feel invisible, ignored, or emotionally unheard. Through raw stories and powerful reflections, this book reminds us that being truly seen and understood can change everything.

Every Moment Counts...invites you to pause, reflect, and realign with what's truly important. Through soulful insights and gentle truth-telling, this book helps you step out of survival mode and into a life of intention, presence, and purpose.

I'm Ready Too!...This powerful guide shines a light on the emotional struggles men face when taught to hide their feelings. Through raw honesty and healing insights, *I'm Ready Too!* helps men break free from emotional silence, reconnect with their truth, and build deeper, healthier relationships. A must-read for any man ready to grow - and for those who love him.

The Do Book...s your wake-up call, your battle cry, your no-excuses guide to finally starting what you've been putting off. Whether it's launching that business, writing that book, going to the gym, or just making a move on a long-delayed dream - this short, sharp, and soul-stirring read will help you stop waiting and start doing.

From the Mind to the Hand...s your wake-up call, your battle cry, your no-excuses guide to finally starting what you've been putting off. Whether it's launching that business, writing that book, going to the gym, or just making a move on a long-delayed dream - this short, sharp, and soul-stirring read will help you stop waiting and start doing.

In **No Help Like Self Help** : Change Your Mind, Change Your Path, Noah takes you through his own journey of chasing success while battling obstacles like comparison, fear, and the infamous "Age Game." Through raw stories and powerful reflections, he reveals how he learned to replace poor thoughts with rich ones, give up on giving up, and step into the freedom of being his best self.

TA4UPublications.com

Made in the USA
Monee, IL
04 November 2026

67378723R10046